VALERIE GILLIES is the author of
recipient of a Creative Scotland A
burgh Makar, poet laureate to the
held writing fellowships in several
Royal Literary Fellow. Currently, she is an Associate of Harvard University. She facilitates the workshops in Creative Writing and the Journaling courses at Maggie's Cancer Centre, Edinburgh.

Praise for work by Valerie Gillies:

Gillies' poetry shows a masterly fluency with form – ballads, haiku, sonnets… This is polyglot poetry, yet it has a remarkably unbookish and outdoors feel. S.B. Kelly

My world is with people, classrooms, hospitals and buildings. I need guides that aid me in flying out of myself to locations that can inform and stretch my world. Valerie Gillies is such a guide. Ted Bowman

Valerie Gillies writes like the wind and jinks like a hare in the fields of language. Candia McWilliam

I like the way these poems are rooted in the elemental world… the craft and the truth are at one. Robert Nye

Energy, cool controlled energy… the classic qualities of the best traditional poetry. Christopher Rush

She is a strong and eloquent celebrant of events and places in the historical and spiritual story of Scotland. She does for Scotland what George Trevelyan did for England – she's a keeper of the Matter of Scotland, a spiritual steward of the meaning of the place, the 'genius loci'. Gabriel Millar

There's such a range to her, she's got a lovely range. Anne Smith

By the same author:

Poetry
Each Bright Eye (Canongate, 1977)
Bed of Stone (Canongate, 1984)
Tweed Journey (Canongate, 1989)
The Chanter's Tune (Canongate, 1990)
The Ringing Rock (Scottish Cultural Press, 1995)
The Lightning Tree (Polygon, 2002)
The Spring Teller (Luath, 2008)

Prose and Poetry
Men and Beasts: Wild Men and Tame Animals of Scotland with photographer Rebecca Marr (Luath, 2000)

The Cream of the Well

New and Selected Poems

VALERIE GILLIES

Luath Press Limited

EDINBURGH

www.luath.co.uk

First published 2014

ISBN: 978-1-910021-68-2

The paper used in this book is recyclable. It is made
from low chlorine pulps produced in a low energy, low emission
manner from renewable forests.

Printed and bound by Bell & Bain Ltd., Glasgow.

Typeset in 11 point Sabon

For Alexia, Calum, Seòras, Nuala and Sorley

Contents

from *Tweed Journey* (1989)

from *The Chanter's Tune* (1990)

from *The Ringing Rock* (1995)

from *Men and Beasts* (2000)

from *The Lightning Tree* (2002)

from *The Spring Teller* (2008)

Uncollected Poems

Acknowledgements

I owe a debt of gratitude to Rebecca Marr, Robyn Marsack, Kendall Dudley, Walter Elliot, Alec Finlay, Ming Chen, Anna S. King, Laura Severin, Jennie Renton and the late Gavin Wallace.

In addition, my thanks go to my publisher Gavin MacDougall, to the curators of the Peabody Museum of Archaeology and Ethnology, to the Department of Celtic, Harvard University, and to Bob Stymeist and all the American birders who shared their knowledge with me in the field.

Without the generosity of Creative Scotland, this book would not have come into being. Moreover, I often think of how my husband, children and grandchildren make space for poetry in their lives.

Traditionally, the 'cream of the well' was the first sip of the well taken at sunrise, when the healing properties of the water were believed to be most potent. People would sleep out all night close to the well, and then they would drink as the sun came up.

from *Each Bright Eye* (1977)

The Gun

Your handsomeness will not relinquish
its poem; it never puts a finish

to the captive words, but hobbles them
until their feel for freedom deadens.

Sight and balance coordinate the whole
of you, you aim with nerved control.

You keep both eyes open and follow through
the arc of the poem's flight, to bring it low.

Marked, maimed, but not yet killed,
the poem shakes a fettered will,

admires your hammerless uncluttered line,
the gunmetal hardness of your mind,

and with an appropriateness of silver
makes overture of peace's quiver.

It attempts to chase the straight stock
of your smooth beauty, to silver its shot

and to damascene the surface
of your bright body. But

your handsomeness will not relinquish
its poem; while it fires, it vanquishes.

Deerhounds

Long dogs, you move with air
belling the vault of your ribcage.
You subdue the miles below your hocks.

Levelled out in speed across wayless country,
over the open grassmoor that is paradise,
the onset of your going undulates the ground.

The bracken hurdles below your height,
the rushes make way for you;
your hard eyes hold in sight the rapid hills.

Brace of deerhounds, a matched two!
Intent, all flame, is what quickens
those long throats thonged with leather.

The Crookmaker

One day it would come into my grandfather's mind
to make a crook and staff.
A shepherd friend had sent
rams' horns for him to give the proper shape.

First, he looked through Scotland's woods
for the single stock in a spread of trees
as far as Blair Atholl, rejecting stick after stick,
looking for the straightest hazel bough.

Then there were days, maybe three,
of turning the incurved twists of the horn
into the single crooked claw of their hooked form,
to one smooth bend like a unique curl of hair.

It unbent through steeping in hot water.
He used his vice-grip to hold it to the curve.
He carved and whittled it to an adorned head,
a curving salmon-leap or a fluffed thistle-top.

He bound crook and staff with loops
of a thick turk's-head knot,
a red turban of twine. All this time
he had never noticed his other walks or work.

But the longest time of all was to come,
smoothing and polishing the crook,
adding each day to its sheen, from
the first emery paper to the last chamois leather.

It changed from angry ruts to fondled silks.
He put on the ferrule last,
tipped the wood with a metal tip,
signing it as of a man's making.

With the finishing stroke put to the work
there sprang up before our eyes
a bough with new proportions,
sprouting a curly horn, blossoming a carving.

The heap of shavings
was still fresh at his feet:
my grandfather not a moment older
through all these days of crook-making.

Mountain Blaw

When I came into my own
it was at some seven years old
going to the Mountain Blaw farm
in a barren cold.

Its roofs were long as a javelin,
a projectile poised by the winter wind,
lying on the ruck of the ridge for muscle,
that shoulder ruche-pleated by streams in ice-hustle.

The house smoked up strange fantail doves
composed of snow; to a fledgling poet
it read as a first draft attempt at love,
steaming out its opacity kettle-hot.

Old bee-skeps and the cows in byre
spelled milk and honey would be there.
The steading looped like briar in a figure-eight
to twine me with my whereabouts that night.

With storm-lamp and pail of hot bran mash
I went into the dark black as horse-treacle
To feed the new grey racing mare, our first.
But outside the loose-box, something quicksilver fickle

– the farm itself – rose sudden as mercury
through a vein, a sense of place saturating
me. Face radiant, the halter held upward of my hand,
I ran home, a spy returned from that promised land.

Letter to Scotland

The hill has a life of its own.
Fish! fish! It whales its way
through the sky,
dashing clouds off
with the temper
of a granite fin.

The hill owns its life.
Dog! dog! it ripples a collar
of pine-studs,
bristles its pinbones
through bracken;
mist froths its jowls.

The Rain Prince

Sheet lightning of an evening
lights the jungle from rich dark.

The first damp of the year
claps to wake a thousand flying-foxes.

Thunder groans and butts its horns,
the impassioned start of bucks.

Clouds downpour upon an hourgreen dust,
the moment's gallop and the musk of deerherds.

These creatures thrive by rainfall,
they hustle and press through the forest.

Sheared off by thunderbolt
their progeny shall be sturdy,

for so they ask their native prince,
the albino elephant, the lord in light rosespots.

An elephant is a rain cloud
who walks on earth.

He is cloud-fabricating,
a monument in grey, binding monsoonclouds.

He conjures his fellow-monsoon
to approach, by whiteness irresistible.

The albino tosses and turns the hills,
for without him the grassblade sleeps.

Stars are Suns

By day, they are hidden in the lit air,
air which scatters light over the whole sky.

Soon after sunset one shines in the west.
Soon before sunrise shines another in the eastern sky.

One may be a sun star, one a dark planet;
they approach from both directions.

Here we might take observations of them,
but what navigator chooses bearings by their latitude?

My worldly heart alone finds them akin to it,
and asks them now to turn away men's wrath.

Most of all, to the planet I address myself,
she differs from the true star, and is my patron:

she gives off no light of her own, shines only
because she reflects his light falling on her.

When these bodies, whitehot and heavenly,
fall through the air to earth,

their reputation begins to make
men turn and look back as they pass.

The Design

Watch how love's oppression
forces me to wording you.
The poem has a surrender in it.

I have tried to use it
to sketch a map of the countries
that I envision in your bed.

I could not trace on its skin
the rock veined with rose quartz
set in deep as your sinews.

Through the flat of my hand
I acquaint myself with that smoothness,
its wellknit sufaces like yours.

On here I'll try each word
with a bold vigilance
– so the Pict drew on stoneface

the line of wolf's breastbone
outjutting,
the line of wolf's loin, loping.

He put down that free flow
by chiselling, and so I know there
must be some wording to fit you.

Fellow Passenger

Mister B. Rajan, diamond buyer,
crystallises from this travelling companion.
He goes by rail, it seems, by criss
and cross, Hyderabad to Bangalore
to Madras, Madras, Madras,
seeking the industrial diamond.

He brings new orient gems from hiding.
Himself, he wears goldwealthy rings
of ruby, and, for fortune,
another of God Venkateswaran.
His smile is a drillpoint diamond's,
incisive his kindness.

Sparrowboned, he walks unstable passageways,
living on boiled eggs and lady's-fingers
with noggins of whisky to follow.
He dreams of his house, the shrineroom picture
of Sai Baba, corkscrew-haired young saint.
And he has at home beautiful hidden daughters.

The Ermine

Cub, you curl in your first sleep
since birth, creaking as a hinge would too
if it were link and bracket
of the two worlds, like you.

A mother so vigilant,
bolt nightlong upright
and wakeful atop a snowbank of starch
I grow pale as winter camouflage fur turns white.

So stoatlike, I hold my head up,
always presenting the face
to you, polecat's young,
where you lie landwide as innocence.

Embroidered on the lining
of my left sleeve, at a glance
I seem to wear the eyes and ears
of ermine, signifying vigilance.

For a Son's First Birthday

You were a Moses striking rock.
I let out the life
that wanted to come.

What I forget
is that restiveness:
there was the true childbed.

I watched the back of your head arrive:
that much form
let me know you were a son.

No bald pate, but a full head of hair;
the appearance of your scalp unfolding
the reality of a new mind within.

Born wringing wet as the moorlands,
you were blue
as blaeberry behind their leaves.

Your first breath
blew you up so pink
you were ragged robin in the marshes.

What I forget
is your first sound:
loud, brilliant and reedy.

from *Bed of Stone* (1984)

Horse Fever

Think over this rough field:
childhoods get spent
among its horses and horizons.

A boy who clings to the old place
can try to sit the forbidden stallion,
that grey from the hilltop farm

whose hoof caught his master's head
the day the small mare was served:
our future is easily over-reached.

Fit mount for some tribesman
with a musket and coxcomb hair,
not for this would-be hero

whose eyes have streamed
and swollen with fever since
he first clapped hand to the saddle.

My small son on the stallion
has one eye gone,
the other almost.

He halts, and grins
from a Tartar horseman's face.
The narrow slits show some sight yet.

This hetman of the Cossacks
reaches manhood, he's staying on
to draw on a chocolate cigarette.

The Mask

A fox with narrow face
runs up our stair
to lie on the dark landing,
looking down.

This is, I think, my daughter
wearing her fox mask,
when all she does
turns to fox.

The reddish-white disk
moves in the shadow, then snaps:
she lets it be known
what she is.

What was once pasteboard
painted and fixed by string
to cap her head
becomes real vixen.

Cut apertures shine
with artful eyes inside:
she's mistress now of subtle wiles
and stinking brush.

She goes in disguise
as a whelp of the wilderness,
she covers her face
to open her heart.

A Fish

The dead sea-fish,
trawled and drowned,
fixes its gape
like a white-and-black newspaper
lockjawed in a letter-box.

If it weren't for that
mouth it makes,
this dead fish could be
the report of beauty.

A Child's Song in the City

Continuous as cities are,
my days have walls on:

home is two houses knocked into one
and the street is a thick crust outside.

Though I learnt my steps
on a staircase of worn stone,

and though I learnt my colours
from the cars filing past,

sometimes I get an orange
and when I'm peeling it

and I see inside,
then I am the first.

Or, wading in the long gutter,
making its waves go,

I am the first
to do so.

Bantam

He's a bantam cockerel
in a speckled jumper,
hotly disputing
each move the other boys make.

A little boy from the street
whose hair bristles like feathers
tied up in the war-bonnet
of a cockerel's crest and comb.

His gymshoe frays on a spurred foot
first in the flurry of kicks.
His punches wing to the heads
of friends and enemies alike.

No matter how big they seem
he is up and at them
as a brief fight bursts out:
bantams battering above long grass.

Damp, volatile after the swimming-pool,
his fingers point like spikes.
Pie-crust juts from his beak,
his eye a black cock's eye.

Bird energy flaps his clothes,
his ragged towel tailing him in the skirmish:
when he's run on,
it lies motionless as a feather.

The Look-Alike

I was asleep when the guest came.
Today he is a man sitting at our table
talking of open boats and million-pound trawlers.

I see the way he moves his hand and head.
It reminds me of you,
it has me loving him instantly.

He tells about the big herring, with scales,
taken in the drift net; but I am seeing you,
right to the cut of your hair.

How could he look like you
when this whole world cannot hold or satisfy me?
Send me the kind of smile I like.

I am setting out the cups
when the kitchen door shuts on my forehead
and I dream stars.

I see you, only you, with a clarity
that feels more passionate to me
than the laughter or the cry of any other man.

The Black Bike

Wearer of a blue Afghan turban
above magnificent features,
he kept on the old warlike look.

He became my best friend.
He'd made up his mind about that
when we met, riding on the racecourse.

Changing from horse to motorbike
gives the balance a queer turn.
My knees had to stop gripping.

For a year we roamed the south
on the black Norton together,
my crash-helmet an oven.

We saw the mosque from the outside
and that field where a Parsee pulled
my father from the fiery wreck in '42.

Yes, I had a great view of India:
it was all your broad back, Manzoor,
and villagers waving to the black bike.

Hound Leaping

The hound Joyous
waits on our threshold.
Late at night
her master opens the door.
She floats toward him,
buoyant, for him to catch her.

She lies out on the air,
the breadth of her brisket lifts her
like a hawk hunting with hanging feet.
She glides in, mouth open,
her slip of pink tongue showing:
the one red tile
in the whole hound mosaic.

Inscription

Through the big field
go two cockerels,
the black and the silver:
they strut up and down,
simple as a Koran verse
lettered in no other colours
than black and silver
and hung on a bleached wall.

Their cock-crow is like
pipes, the cry to prayer.

They pass by
with their three hens.

If you do come back
you won't find the same field again,
you won't find them.

Dipping

When the ice breaks, we come to the river,
throwing stones, not dice, hoping
for the throw that zigzags, the splash
that forms again. The spawn
flows where you spat,
it creams on a slipping wave.
We dip in the water but stand up
while birds go by laid flat in flight
and the fishes lie along to swim.
We turn to the cold and stony shore.
How two sisters can stay together
appears to us, with our lovers along,
like foam caught frozen at the fall.

Chilcarroch Farmsteading

A moorland farm grows out of the hillside.
Where is it hewn stone? Where is it native rock?
The house is withdrawing from the eye, yet is the presence
of the high fields and the granite boulders there.

Its long grey roof follows the line of the hill;
winds sing at those slates when trees are leafless.
All its outhouses, stable, byre and calving shed
are built as coverings for a living contiguity,
the up and the across of them touch in one sober tint
variegated by blotches, under the influence of weather.

Inhabited from father to son by men of one occupation,
whose work waited only for the lark,
the moor house is strength formed in itself.
Each recess, each projection in its walls or roofs,
from the strong lintel to the thick stone porch,
those granite boulders simply split,
shows the true substance of defence, here,
where wind flows from a height and air changes into rain.

See in Chilcarroch a stone that's freshly turned up,
which by colour and by shape must call to mind
only these hills, and how they stand round to be named.

from *Tweed Journey* (1989)

The Rant of the Trows

From weirs and caulds to streamy pools,
The rocky foss past, come famous casts,
By Orchard Heads to Nethern Heads:
The Side Straik and Elshie Stream,
The Red Stane, the Laird's aim,
The Dark Shore, the noble Doors,
A rippling reach, tough fins in each,
With a brisk curl on the water's whirl.

By turmoil, rapid and the flat,
The out-bring will snap and sing
Through deep Trows, the rare Trows.

A wizard's foot set the current's root,
The print of it in the gorge gullet
An active lad might leap dryshod.
Who lacks belief comes to grief
In the slit defile, a devil's smile,
The four troughs deep enough,
The narrow Trows, the rapid Trows.

The rock rent, the torn vents
Fling a bar, form a scar
Of cleft kerb, the stone curb
Where time is nicked to the quick
By sharp Trows, the bare Trows.

The ardent rate concentrates
The whole force to gush hoarse
To say it, to vary wit

In water vow from bold pow.
The trap rock, the pelt shock
Rings the Trows, scotch-snap Trows,
Makerstoun's Trows below Mertoun.

Pressen Hill

Somewhere here, there's water still to find,
contained in earth's crust from earlier geologic time.
True connate water is very rare,
as if a pyramid had trapped the ancient air.
Who would breathe it, who would drink
the element held within its brink?
And breathing, drinking, broach for us then
the first word of the biosphere to men.

The Canto of Tweed's Mouth

Walking from source to sea
draws a lifeline's journey.
Spray spread
on my head,
foam on my body,
I leave it on me.
Well-drinker, bank-walker, my boat
is ottering down on the river's long rope.

Tueda, who has one of the old names,
so old there's no meaning to explain,
you know it's a suspicious time, we sue
those who boil the oceans down for glue
and we fear the glassful from the tap.
Swallow our despair, rise up,
open your mouth, the origin of things,
the first voice to speak or sing,
foretell fresh water for us,
bearer of youths and of harvests.
Brand your flood-shape into the rocks,
turn full-face to us, wavy locks.

'Far from me, Tweedsmuir,
the midmoss of man's cure,
far from me, Fruid and Quair,
the first waters of Scotland there.'

By braided channel, riverbed of the brain,
man and land she plaits again,
slows to a big lowland waterway

where pool and rapid die away.
Tides back the water up, centuries of war
cross the narrow haven's shallow bar,
sea-wealth under bastion and parapet,
the water-walls of beleaguered Berwick.

Give her the love-talk of the names,
colours brought down in spate's champagne.
From long Slake to old Scotsgate,
Hang-a-dyke Neuk and Longheughs,
slip and quays, Gillies Braes,
groynes and piers, Breakneck Stairs,
Calot Shad for diving shag,
Back Gut Stell and Conqueror's Well,
to the last land, Out Water Batt,
Tueda's fish-mouth opens for that.
She lifts her head from the nets, flows
by and touches us as she goes.

From the uplands and high moors
to the broad valley and seashores,
space! And the river signs her course:
form is the diagram of force.
Water propels a wave, an impetus;
whatever is in nature, is also in us.

Play the note and say her name
before the world shall change again,
ruined it can never be
while Tweed runs to the sea.

from *The Chanter's Tune* (1990)

The Mugdrum Sequence

for Derek Robertson

(i)

River Island
from Dante's *Purgatorio*, Canto 1, lines 100–105

Questa isoletta intorno ad imo ad imo,
là giù colà dove la batte l'onda,
porta dei giunchi sovra il molle limo:
null'altra pianta che facesse fronda
o indurasse, vi puote aver vita,
però che a le percosse non seconda.

All around this little island in its reaches low
down there where the wave is beating,
tall reeds from soft mud can grow:
no other plant can live there, bearing
leaves or hardening in its prime,
that will not bend when tides are battering.

(ii)

The Death of Adonis

Three go through the world,
boar, hound and man.
Blood anemones
redden the slopes after rain.

(iii)

Reed Harvest

Pancake flat, plank of gold,
little tuft, reeds and rushes,
channel changer, moving shallows,
the islandman, a life fisher,
the island goddess sways the flood.

Solid stone, fluid river,
yellow eyot within the firth,
by stone pillar and low hill
an islet stands, a small world,
a dry site at sea level.

A brazen boar, a ridgeback,
beast of the chase, wood sense;
in mudbank the boat of oak,
a dugout canoe, boar openmouthed,
the eyeboat is preserved in mud.

Duckshooter trapped waderheight,
shotgun repeats at twilight tide,
shouts and cries on true bank,
a boar swims to the island,
a tusky one to Mugdrum.

(iv)

After Mugdrum

View now and see
the Mugdrum stone:
when this is gone,
so shall we be.

Get us an amulet,
a horn to form one piece with the helmet.
The most effective for us to survive
is a tusk taken while the boar is alive,
the boar who was a king,
Silver Bristle: like silver wings
those glittering bristles show the path
he takes through the forest in his wrath.

In the greatest wind in the world
a smoke is blowing south, unfurled
and not being turned, you understand,
by the skies or over land.
That is the fire on shore
where a huntsman singes a wild boar.

On the stone, a hunting frieze:
horsemen and boars together
are too far weathered
for certainty.

Here they left a message for us
we cannot read without the tusk:
how that hunting-party ended,

what hound a chieftain's life defended
as through them all one boar rushed free,
swam the Tay and out to sea.

(v)

The Mugdrum Strathspey

Carpow and Mugdrum,
Gillies Burn, Mugdrum,
Wester Clunie, Mugdrum,
Skirlbear, Mugdrum,

Abernethy, Mugdrum,
Sweerie, Mugdrum,
Lumbennie, Mugdrum,
Whinnybank, Mugdrum.

Butter Well, Mugdrum,
Pow of Lindores, Mugdrum,
Clatchard Craig, Mugdrum,
Denmylne, Mugdrum.
Tay and Earn, Mugdrum,
Tay and Earn, Mugdrum.

The fighting men of Carpow ground,
        a horseman caught in mud,
the baited boar with foamy tusk,
        fishers swept away by flood,
they seek the shifting Wonder Bank
        where snouts of water tug.

The curved tusk at the new moon
    meets swordblade on The Hard,
his narrow eye sees all the ways
    but the Kerewhip Bank's a star:
the man who wears the sheet-bronze scales
    has skin without a scar.

Fruid Water

Tune: 'Logan Water'

Fruid Water, furthest of all from the sea,
yours is the voice that means far more to me
than the salty wave flowing up the beach
of a great stretch of ocean I may never reach.
Little I care for foaming breakers on the shore
or the surface calm that moves so much slower
if I hear your notes that are sweeter than the surf
of all the different waters of the earth.

I don't need to see the whale or sea-wrack,
the fight of the gannet, the diving of the shag,
I long to watch your trout, or your owl flying low,
on your banks I hear the sudden hooves of the roe.
Each of us finds that you can quench our thirst,
stream and surrounding terrain belong together from the first.
In the face of the light you become, through your quality,
like an eye reflecting us in transparency.

Huge masses of water roll in the oceans,
deep currents circulate, of gigantic proportions,
but where you flow freely and trickle over stones
you play with waves in rhythm, vibrate and sing alone.
Out of vapour you have come back to liquid,
you return in your course every time to Fruid.
Evaporating, loop with air currents and precipitate:
between earth and heaven you mediate.

Your moving form issuing from the hills
twists in strands of water changed like turning veils;
they make a rope that spirals down the glen,
new water falling though it to refresh men.
I can tell by the current as it swirls along
where it comes from, what rocks cause its tension,
and I praise your wave shapes through which the water flows,
for they remain the same, and rarely go.

Harp Music

from the Gaelic of Sileas na Ceapaich

Welcome back, clarsach,
  Since I put you away firmly;
Now if I could keep you in
  You wouldn't go out in a hurry.

Melodious the ribbed tidebank of strings
  Being tuned up so near;
I am overjoyed by your yellow sweet body
  Played close by my ear.

If I were a rich heiress
  You would always be around to sing;
I would hear you make love to me
  After waking in the morning.

Dearer than fiddle or bass,
  Organ or any instrument, I'm sure,
My choice beyond all other music
  Your strings sounding through firm hard boards.

Young Harper

Above Tweed Green levels
Maeve first raises the harp.

Prosper her hand that plucks
then clenches fist like a jockey.

Grip inside thighs
the colt with a cropped mane.

Turn blades on the curved neck
bristling with spigots.

Out from the rosewood forest
came this foal of strung nerve.

Stand in your grainy coat,
let her lift elbows over you.

Keep her thumbs bent
and fingers strong to do the playing.

Eight summers made them, clarsach,
I freely give you my elder daughter.

Girls on a Swing

The girls are swinging
together on the plastic seat
in the mid-light evening.

The arbour is made of pleated peach
twinned trees, on these
one bird is perched for each.

The girls' swinging so light
is the rising and setting of the moon,
its semi-circular flight.

They hold ropes of orange yarn:
their young faces
turn on the wind's charm.

Wherever they fly,
wherever they look, they fructify
the garden, fruit trees and the sky.

William Johnstone, Farmer and Artist

As I go to my studio I hear my father saying, sadly, 'Ah, Johnstone, think what a great farmer you might have been!'
Last words of his autobiography, *Points in Time*

His eye travels over
the line of the Pictland bull
and makes out the mass and weight
by his sense of design and space:
the same eye singles out
Bardolph, perfect in his conformation,
to stand at Satchells farm.

His mind moves around
cult animals and wonder beasts
and opens out their form
to his students of the abstract:
the same mind has found
the sheep under the snow
lying like the spokes of a wheel
beneath the rolling rhythm
of the visual field.

The hand that ploughs the first furrow
loads his brush and continues a line:
the furrows become a pattern,
the ground changes colour,
team and man are one with the field.
The earth artist, how he sees things,
lends his meaning to their meaning.

Young Farmer at the Cashmere Goat Sales

He's clean of limb, and his new-shaven chin rests on his hands
That fold over the long crook at throat-height. He stands
In his turned-up hillboots, bestrides this slippery deck,
Colossus in tweeds, with a camera and a thousand-pound cheque.
He moves the crook to stir the beasts about some,
Telling by their big knees if there's more growth to come.

He tries their coats between forefinger and thumb,
The long white topfleeces like a spiral perm.
He feels for the dense handful of cashmere beneath,
Combs the riches per ounce these male kids will bequeath.
A young girl hangs over the corner-rail to hear his jargon:
He reaches a finger to her hair, to gauge the first carding.

Hunter's Mask

He lived alone, up country,
further than the eucalyptus slopes,
higher than one day's coffee blossom.

His verandah perched above
all the southern highland valleys,
the rent and chasm of them.

He wouldn't talk much
or come along with us.
He turned and he looked away.

He lent me
a beautiful gun in its case,
two interlocking pieces.

Loading at a tankbund,
I fitted barrel and stock together:
they were well-oiled, gleaming.

Others told me, years before,
he was on foot in the northern forest
and when he turned round

a bear gripped him by the head.
In the bite of claws and teeth
he kept to one purpose.

He pressed close in its embrace
until his free hand
found his revolver and fired.

Then the bear rampant
fell back, taking
half his face with it.

I saw duck fly, moon rise,
the scrape of the road on the hill.
I cleaned his gun carefully.

'He never lends it out,'
they said. As I was young,
they made me scared to return it.

Going back up to the house,
I thought of that bear-hug.
I regarded his one lunar eye:

the clawmarked bear path,
the wide goggle and strap
on the helmet of his skull,

the frightened and the frightening.
His courage continued
its halfmoon shine, the hunter's mask.

What She Told Her Friend

A variation on the classic Tamil love poem by Venmaniputti, a woman poet of the first century AD.

At a late-night party watched by no-one
who had not been drinking,
in sofas like groves
filled with leaves and birdsong,
on the banks of chintz
clustered with flowers,

I sat in his lap,
my arm around his neck.

My eyes could not see him

it was too smoky
and he got too close

my ears could not hear him

full of his kisses
and snaps of laughter.

But my hand grew beautiful
on his shoulder
and shrivelled to bone
when I took it away.

What am I to make of this?

Shepherd's Calendar

It was after Chernobyl we heard of it,
that they slaughtered all the Lapps' reindeer,
buried a radioactive hundred thousand in a great pit.

While up the Quair Water our lambs were born
with one eye in the middle of their heads,
with no tails or no back passage or weird horns.

It was the same for Greeks after Oedipus,
everything shows the signs of a miasma,
a time when the wrong people are ruling us.

The Ericstane Brooch

The gold cross-bow brooch,
The Emperors' gift to an officer,
Was lost on the upland moor.
The pierced work and the inscription
Lay far from human habitation.

It worked on time and space
And they were at work on it.
What could withstand them?
But it was waiting for the human,
To address itself to a man or woman.

In the wilderness it meant nothing.
The great spaces dissolved its image,
Time obliterated its meaning.
Without being brought in,
It was less than the simplest safety-pin.

Now the brooch is transporting the past
To the present, the far to the near.
Between the two, its maker and wearer
And watcher live mysteriously.
Who is this that values it so seriously?

It exists, it has been seen by him.
If it speaks, it can only say
'He lost me'. And we reply, 'Who?
For he can also be our loss,
This moment floating face-down in the moss.'

Dumb replica: the original is in Los Angeles.
How is it, the man once destroyed,
His brooch continues boundlessly?
Our very existence is what it defies:
We no longer see what once we scrutinized.

The Man in the Moss

There is one marsh nobody reclaims.
Over rusty water, the reedbeds
Trail ochre strips and shreds.
From time to time, a straw will stir
As if someone draws air
Through it, down below the surface again.

Turf banks are riddled by water-voles.
As a girl, I ran along the margin lightly,
Chasing a rabbit between me and the collie.
It shot in below the bank and hid there.
I lay my length, fingertip to fur,
The dog watching my arm in the hot holt.

Then the birse along his back bristled.
The rabbit made off clean as a whistle
While we two saw someone marvellous,
A lad naked in the bog beside us,
Plunging down till only his head showed
Above water, face at an angle of repose,

Regarding us. He lasted it out,
Enduring hunger, thirst, hardship's butt,
Living by hunting, swift of foot,
Knowing the marsh, taking reeds and roots,
Things do not change for him as they do for us:
The dog long dead, I read of tribes in Dio Cassius.

from *The Ringing Rock* (1995)

The Rink

Light plays on the Rink,
on birches in the broch, its outer wall.
You are here with me in silence.

A doe hare comes this way, in no hurry,
not expecting to find humans here,
loping close enough to touch.

Her warm brown back blends
with the feather-grass, her fur
a burr-elm of reds and yellows.

After her come two jack-hares,
one solid, one spindly, following her trail
with twists and turns, tides to her moon.

Most marvellous, moving smoothly,
the run of the hares is the lie of the land.
There are times when the creature is a ghost.

We think they have all gone,
till we turn and look behind us:
in the shadow of a shadow

a golden hare rests in the birchwood,
touched thousands and thousands
of times by the sun.

A Sapling Greyhound

I like to meet my friend the greyhound:
for her, I hang my head upside down
and she takes my ear in her white teeth.
I feel the bite of winter nip the heath.

Intaglio Ringstone

for Walter Elliot

The hill is a globe, and the ploughland,
Well-washed by rainshowers, inswells
Its furrows. Whistling through a blowhole, can
This be a sea-beast surfacing from where it dwells?

A small and perfect dolphin in the stone
Is leaping, with its tail up,
Smooth-skinned, cut into the two-tone
Slate-grey oval, to fit the sardonyx hump.

This good-luck charm goes as one integer
From the engraver's hand, it passes on
By a long-lost man the whole way to its finder.

The beaked dolphin makes its own impression:
It scribes the tides, calls and hears underwater,
Crosses seas and bears a man beyond.

Note: An intaglio is a gem with an incised carving. Here, the gemstone is a sardonyx, with a sunk pattern of a dolphin, lost from a Roman ring and found at Trimontium by Walter Elliot.

Shale Bings

The roads are red, the ground smells raw,
dank soil and air in ironstone country,
the oilshale smelted with coking coal,
bings and farms among rush-choked uplands.

You are the darling place of disused quarries,
dismantled railways, new open-cast mines.
Your rocks, upraised, are worn down again,
buried under the pile of their own ruin.

You lie on the surface of the world,
abandoned on the skin of the earth,
the stacks and jags of red shale
moored among moss-hags and old pits.

You keep bringing up the past.
Motorbike boys are scrambling over the top
when the bing moves beneath them.
A bike turns over: wheels in the drift.

while I was away

you came looking for me
where the deerskin dries on the shed door
and the hound lies out like a rock

you were asking for me
where a steady stream flows past the field
and the rain sounds easy in the grass

you're returning for me
there at night you go by among the trees
and time shifts round like the wind

Viking Boy

a sandstorm strips the dune
to bare bones
on a straw mat
over a bed of feathers
the boy lies
a hoop of metal
shelters his head
the shield over his face
the sword by his flank
he has a bone comb
not a yellow hair in it
the bed to soften
the blow to the boy
the shield to hide
his young face
from the sharp scatter
from the first handful of sand

Bass Rock

The rock punctuates the sealine.
Our boat circles the Bass.
Seals swim beneath us,
pop fruit-machine heads up
three at a time, outstare us.

People press towards them,
lean to starboard all at once.
We lurch below the cliffs.
On their dung-yellow rock,
gannets rest a beak-stab apart.

Strathfillan Sequence

Note

Nicknamed 'little wolf', the Celtic Saint Fillan lived in Glendochart in the eighth century, and miraculous powers are attributed to his relics in folk tradition.

His bell and staff were guarded by hereditary keepers known as dewars. Carried at the coronation of King James IV, *his staff, the Coygerach, is a masterpiece of metalwork encasing the original wooden crook. The dewars of the Coygerach emigrated to a backwoods farm in eastern Canada in the nineteenth century, and the staff stayed with them there for sixty years, while it continued to be used for healing purposes. Eventually, like his bell which had been stolen by an English antiquary, it returned to Scotland.*

Fillan's hand bell had the power of flight and could cure the sick. It was kept in the ruins of his chapel, ready to be used to cure madness. The ritual began with a dip in the Holy Pool and ended after a night spent with the bell placed above the lunatic's head. Saint Fillan's bell and staff can be seen in the National Museum of Scotland.

Now lost, the silver case containing his arm-bone was with Robert the Bruce at the Battle of Bannockburn, and the king attributed his victory there to its miraculous appearance on the preceding night.

Today, cures for many illnesses are attributed to Fillan's healing stones, preserved in the mill at Killin for over a thousand years.

The Bell

Give me a ring
about Saint Fillan's bell

clang clang clank
the beating bell
like pails
like cowbells
cracked and clappered
rings in your ears
goes right through you
its sounding clangour
its loud *clogarnach*
jangling

the *ronnaich*, the poet-bell,
sang songs, rang
to call people
clang clang clank
it cracked on the day
it flew here
it beats all the windy places
it claps time
it has a tongue
rung against thunder
it frees us from danger
by fire or lightning-flash

quadrangular, clang
bronze-clad, clang
dragon-handled, clang
hum tintinnabulum

rung around
its sound creates
its shape hangs
between earth and sky
in the bell-vault
it cures lunatics
the bell flies overhead
a crack of light
rings the changes

cast all in one
hand-bell, mixed metal
though it's carried off
it will return
ringing all the way
grateful to the ear
of the wanderer in the bush
its clang softened by distance
by the intervening forest
its potent *clogarnach*
announces its return
to Saint Fillan's cell
his yellow bell

The Holy Pool

It's dusk and a first quarter moon.
A mad girl shambles on a riverbank
Rotted by rain, splintered by frost,

Wasted by wind and sun. A turf
Loosening, she drops into the water,
Taking a plunge into the holy pool.

At a wide angle of the river
The pool is broad and deep, so clear
You can see the gravel on the bottom.

Fist full of pebbles, her mouth opens,
She looks up through the water:
Wavy figures are peering down at her.

They walked her thirty miles for this.
Her brothers drag her to the surface
By a rope, tight round her waist.

She bobs like a cork, as mad as ever.
Wet and wistful, she carries her stones
To the three cairns, round the lucky way.

It's all happening in the dark, yes,
Under what could be the moon they walk
The half-mile to the ruined chapel.

Her head centred in the heart-shaped stone,
They tie her down, under a wooden frame
Knotted with ropes. Her cries tug,

Covered with straw for the night.
They place Saint Fillan's bell on her head,
A crazy nightcap on the girl.

Alone, she's hearing the riverwave
Whisper of change in its changes of sound:
The pool, the bell, the bell, the pool.

Damp from her face and hair
Condenses on the sides of the bell
And runs down: bell-metal sweats for her.

Inside the bell is inside the pool.
Someone's drawing on the rope,
Bringing her up through four elements:

Pool where the earth-bank holds water,
Bell where fired bronze holds air.
Her eyes open underwater, under light.

At sunrise her brothers return to lift
Off the bell. They see the knots are loose
That tied her body and warped her mind.

Coda: the girl speaks

'My mouth full of water
from the holy pool
I swam in four elements

My mind washed in air
in the shock of the pool
going under Saint Fillan's bell

I saw my dead grandfather
return to help me,
he untied the knots

I am a child of grace
in the chapel of marvels
my reason returns

I make my circuit
in the pool, in the bell,
in the fellowship of my Fillan'

The Coygerach

Across the Atlantic, you're a wanderer
Shining in silver-gilt, a sea-tinker.
        Trapping the bright stick
        Your case becomes as holy as its relic.
In your own land you're a stranger.

The metalworker taps in rivets
Round the small hole of your gullet,
        Core for the crook, the crozier
        Encased in bronze here:
This rifled groove could spin a bullet.

Springs of metal turn around the knop,
A charmstone of crystal in the drop
        Tossed in coil and quoit
        One line visits every point
Chased with silver in a wiry rope.

Wood sunk in a hollow, streamy
Eddies in a spate of filigree
        Show sinuous space is dense,
        Make meaning out of emptiness,
Frost on your marvellous tree.

Human arms are carrying
You to the crowning of our kings.
        Like a girl in her snood,
        You wear your monk's hood,
A cloud aground in your lightning.

Your keepers farmed at Ewich.
A hill with its back up, their relic
        Glittered in a simple croft;
        Shrine with your crest aloft
Like a mountain pony's mane, just as thick.

If your dewar set out on a journey
He had the royal letter, he answered only
        To the king, he could pursue
        Reivers, pass among tribal feuds
Anywhere in Scotland, that's your potency.

People could ask for the cattle cure
Or one for fever in humans, curlicues
        Of water poured through, sprinkled
        On them, given them to drink.
Wherever the Coygerach dips, is pure.

River-curve Coygerach, no-one can stand
Too close to your current coming in to land.
        Liars lose the power to speak,
        Treasure returns with its thief,
You are the light shining from Fillan's hand.

The Night Before Battle

Seeing the wind
before the storm
the king watched Fillan's
miraculous arm
float on its own
through the silver case
till the arm-bone
clakkit into place.

Scotland's pride
at Bannockburn shown,
what mountain hides
his holy bone?
Our saint, our Fillan,
our fate transform,
seeing the wind
before the storm.

The Healing Stones

A child goes to Killin in spring
to Saint Fillan's healing stones:
eight waterworn stones he left us,
then we were on our own.

Gather the Christmas rushes
that have been washed up
by floods upon the riverbank:
they must never be cut.

Stones for each part of the body,
for the head and breast and back,
for the limbs and internal organs,
must rest on fresh riverwrack.

There's a black oval curing-stone
against the child's pain.
'Three times one way, three the other,
now the first way again:

rub it lightly around.'
The child's face flushes red,
her body tingles, from the icy stone
a sensation of heat spreads.

In place, back on their rushbed,
the stones lie, after the spate.
A great flood has swept over them
and over the child, from the saint.

Mother-of-Pearl

‘Was it all right with your mother
when you phoned? Did you tell her
you’d fallen in the Tay
and that you’d found a pearl?’

‘I have a reddish one, and a grey,
but this one is pure white.’
The boy is opening the oyster,
one foot in the wave.

The Hand's Span

Your hand places a dram-glass on the board.
Beyond the window, the river is two miles broad.
On the green knuckles of those North Fife hills
My thistledown kiss can seed where it will.

Easier for me to cross the sea-gravel strand
Than reach out now to take your hand.
I steal a glance while you're looking away:
Tides break on a sandbar in the Tay.

Rope-rough, calloused mariner's palm,
Backhand and wrist on the shipwright's arm
Weathering work with bone, resin or strake:
I love every mark your hand makes.

Better for the birds who take wing with a start
Than the two of us who are waking apart.
The river-mouth flows, at one with the land,
It's not so with me and my kiss on your hand.

from *Men and Beasts* (2000)

Hill Lambing

in homage to John Berger

There's fleece, horns, hooves, grass, breath, mud,
teeth, mash, dung, blood, afterbirth, milk,
lamb jackets and the noise of bleating,
zinc buckets and a bottle of antiseptic,
pens to be cleaned, syringes to be rinsed,
ice on his boots and a light at his window.

The Sealstone of Caracalla

Rain and a light-ray on the nailclip edge of red jasper,
The sealstone found in a field, the finger-mask returns,
My palm-pilot now, sticks to my skin and won't leave me.

You put the intaglio into my hand in the restaurant,
Among voices of the Romagna it morphs into his face.
A loyalty badge, it does his talking for him,

A pager reminding me who I'm lunching with today,
Scrolling through passport-size photos, whoever I want to call.
Two thousand year old stunner, a beauty, the only one

Taking a hold on minds. Rich bloody red
Too right for a tyrant, his hairstyle an Elvis quiff,
Caracalla was a real rocker in his designer cloak.

On a killing spree he murdered his brother Geta
In front of his mother. A crazy gambler with a passion
For the Blues *factio*, he bet on all the star charioteers.

This tiny likeness blows up into a gross icon
With the sense of his own status. It's the red clue,
The head crossing my hand, o intaglio hello,

Tell where you've been and who you know.
I have been below the engraver's copper wheel
And the soldering torch where his hair smouldered.

Electric Deerhounds

Two deerhounds play in the field, they wire
it by themselves. Volts jump across the air
between them. They're plugged in to Bizzyberry Hill,
currents flow through the filaments of their hair.
Tungsten coats. Animal magnetism. They thrill,
the visible charge. Creatures of heaven, they fill the eye.

A Year's Work

the rush of lambing
the driving of ewes
the speaning of lambs
the dipping of flocks
the keeling of ruddles
the war against maggots
the clipping at the fank
the walking of hills
the selling of shearlings
the gathering of a hirsel
the dressing of sticks
the quiet of the back-en'

Clydesdale Clydesdale

Flanks of the hill fall sharply to the bank,
a bend in the river. The summit, the withers.
The scarp line, the crest of a mane.

River-valley, a broad back. Home pastures
where grass, soil, moisture,
everything helps to grow a good horse.

Light wands waver through slatted sheds.
The dark colt turns blacker,
a white blaze runs down his face.

The Brow Burn shines beside fertile rises.
Somewhere near, there's the bronze figurine
of a horse still to discover.

from *The Lightning Tree* (2002)

A Lightning Print

Cloud-to-ground cracks its long spark,
it kills one in every six it strikes.

I break the lightning like a bell,
it goes around the outside of me,

it jumps the gap, it leaps,
I'm changed for ever.

My mouth is full of silver
and I can't even spit it out.

A whiff of smoke rises off my scalp:
scorchmarks on my soles,

the feet swivel round on my heels,
my back becomes my breast.

A photo of my surroundings
appears on my skin;

there's a glow around my hand.
I treasure life every day,

I love the lightning,
I walk out and I watch it.

Lepus

Sit tight. Flow into the ground
as if skin and bone are melting.
Get smaller as you're approached.
If that stone diminishes, it's you.

After a wet summer, when the cover
grows thick, sit in your own shape
till you're almost trodden on.
Move off, leaving your form still warm.

In a dry summer, when the grass
is thin and sparse, and already
you've travelled far by night,
shift off out of slipping distance.

Hug the shoulder of a hill.
Go around to rest, circling
in the lee of the wind.
Bring the sun onto your back.

Weird being without feather or wing
lie out in the frost, live on
at the limits of the uplands,
wild hare folding into fog.

Be there in all the same places
you always are, Orion following
you across the sky fields.
Run on, lang lugs, take me with you.

Runway Lights

where jets are taking off or landing
the wild hares teem

while noisy aircraft are taxiing round
hares cruise stiff-legged

near engines roaring like thunderclaps
they skip in the air

the hares who were here before we appeared
love the storm

the hares who can hear our footfall vibrate
they like the airport

they race alongside at take-off
trying to overtake

they run in the passengers' sight
we watch them

– cleft lips, fluffed cheeks, side-set eyes –
they watch us

each individual varies in colour and shape
hares vary as humans do

racing for the sun-gates, no time to pass
the dew-hoppers run

through a point separating every here from there
the hares lead the way

Singing the Storm

for Savourna Stevenson

I'll never arrive
on moving land
in shifting skies
I need the map
of another planet

No valley or hill
no roads, no cars
in a white shell
I'm hearing the sea
who's hidden the stars?

Snow seeks a form
a flock of ice
runs in the storm
a dark shepherd
whistles and drives

Someone's going by
in the wind
where the wayward
bird dies
and the cold begins

It ends on a note
gusty and hollow
I take off
my coat
for a pillow

Singing the storm
going to sleep
now I can dream
it's getting warm
beneath the sheets

I go out through my smile
I follow the snow
mile after mile
I go with
the wind and snowdrift

Suave Dancer

The starved lightning chose Suave Dancer,
famous racehorse in his paddock outside Melbourne,
the stallion among the mares, siring dreams,

 the current travels through his hooves.

The shadow of a hungry bird falls on his face.
Race the horse of the sky against the horse of the earth,
the traveller in the wind is lost in the morning

 before the sacrifice of a colt to the year.

The pure-bred horses see him for a long time.
Under the horse-tree of his veins the stallion stands
in his own shade and the lightning lifts a horse's skull

 and other omens are on the way.

Ivor Gurney at Bangour

Ivor Gurney, poet. With Gloucesters in France, 1916. Gassed near Passchendaele; sent to Bangour War Hospital, autumn 1917. Died, London asylum, 1937. Complete poems published, 1954.

It's always that spooky light in November,
the winter lightlessness. He liked that too,
Ivor, an inmate here, a trench-companion.

The hospital had its own station, then.
Three short blasts on the steam hooter to say
the ambulance train was arriving in darkness.

Stretcher-bearers at the shed with lamps
lit. Alerted by telegram, *300 tonight.*
Some sitting, some lying prone, fever cases,

or with gassing and shellshock. Like Ivor.
Tents for the thousands of angry amputees.
Tree-stumps in the leaf-litter woods,

plane and lathe in the peg-leg workshop,
a basket wheelchair with a headlamp. Now
it's tossed out on the skip. Under floorboards

lie a stack of glass negatives, medical photos
of head injuries, warriors' faces blown away.
Birch trees erupt through the station platform.

St Fillan's Crook

A stranger to its native strath,
the tall foreigner, the *coygerach*
was at the crowning of our kings,
raised the crest of all bright things.

Its keeper went to eastern Canada,
he carried the crook, the nomad,
to use its crystal as a cattle cure.
Where it dips, the water's pure.

From Canadian forests, settlers sent
the wanderer back into its element,
silver stripes crossing the Atlantic.
The brightness is inside the relic.

I am Speaking to my Saint

I am speaking to my saint
in the dark and in the day
in months of light and shade
        Fillan my love

the frost never touches you
the sun stands still for you
the earth rises under you
        your shadow heals

your bell flies in the day
it goes ringing all the way
to one named for our lady
        curing her fever

saint of the bronze bell
saint of the holy pool
saint of the silver crook
        come to my child

saint of the shining hand
saint of the armbone
saint of the healing stones
        help cure her

saint of the serried hills
saint of Glendochart's cell
in your chapel of marvels
        take away her pain

saint of the mountain pass
saint of the curved staff
a river bend around the lass
        keep her well

in the deep pool she's dipping
give grace to the living
on your rock she's landing
        Fillan my love

breathe life into her mouth
all the cold will go out
of the water that you touch
        Fillan, see my Màiri

Golden Breast

'Say goodbye to your breast,' she said,
'for tomorrow it will be gone.'

So I walked far into the hills.
I opened my shirt,
the sun set on my breast.

Next day, the tissue
the surgeon cut
and the pathologist placed
between slides,
that wasn't the golden breast
on the hill
in a place where light stays.

Cool Cap

You couldn't have a serious conversation
with anyone who looks like me
under the cool cap during chemotherapy.

A cobalt-blue two-layered helmet
like a Woman-in-the-Wind biker wears,
the cap comes out of the freezer. Icecrust on it.

When the great wave comes crashing
and the chemicals rush to my scalp
the cap stops my hair falling out.

The freezing layer caps the globe.
I'm under the permafrost, it's preserving
this nomad woman with her six horses.

Here's my needle tattoo on kidskin, my weird
colour hair, my strange crescent headgear.
Let in today's air, I melt away,

fading out the derby-day trampling beat
of those wild gallops on the high plateau,
the grip of this hard hat thawing.

A Few Haiku

out comes the sun
wind blows up over the hill
– kite flying a boy

sometimes forgetting
put his tea on the table
beside the others

wet to our skins
our black umbrella waving
no taxi stops

all night long
moon kept coming in and out
no-one lost the place

storm is fishing
the thunder-and-lightning fly
black with an orange streak

Norman Iain Sorley George
Scalpay Lewis Raasay Hoy
each poet an island

sit on the platform
buoyed up on bare boards
– palomino horse

The Space Between Us

In his glen one song always goes on air
Round the lip of Corrie Vanoch, where I first heard it.
I see him everywhere I look, a moving figure,
Spring-heeled he walks the slopes, leaps the stream,
And he speaks from the well-head of Tobar a' Chinn.

When I follow the pass upwards towards Monega,
Time is running by me with a sleety kiss
And a footprint appears in new snow beside mine.
If I turn round suddenly in the fields of his farm,
His gaunt good looks are easily seen on Craig Soilleur.

Over the high ridge of Cuingard I hear the storm
Eddy through cliff and cleft like a windpipe,
While his song keeps on coming, a torrent
That never stops flowing through the ravine.
The space between us takes shape where he calls
On love, in the breezeway of Glen Isla's sonic seam.

Maeve in Manhattan

She's the sibyl of silver
the prophet of platinum
techno diva in titanium
she's the goldsmith girl

long nights in the studio
welding at a workbench
going gem-cutting
with jewellers in Jaipur

she's enamelling in India
powder-coating spun copper
like a Ducati motorbike
she's metalworking in Manila

turns her lathe in typhoons
drives to live volcanoes
scuba-dives to corals
the goldsmith girl

closes vice and clamp
zaps her Zag toolbox
on files and fretsaws
silver scrap and ring shanks

the girl comes and goes
with her fibre-optic neckpiece
flashing stellar galaxies
pricing precious metals

she rollerblades to work
creating catwalk jewellery
kinky kinetic
slinky prophetic

alien abduction
astral seduction
starry nights in gold and steel
the goldsmith girl

The Sitooterie

a little way
from house or school
is the hidden hut
at a distance from it all

a log cabin
built of douglas fir
longlasting
here or elsewhere

you make a stay
go on retreat
where you look for shade
beneath a leaf

heat or cold
set no limit
for hand-cut timber
not a nail in it

the bluetit nests
in the crabapple tree
a butterfly sunning
takes time to be

with tap and patter
the wind picks up
rain pelts the roof
runs in the water butt

trace a raindrop
with your finger
you follow on foot
two great rivers

stand in the doorway
looking out
– step towards the world
or back into the hut?

a passing blackbird
sees you sitting still
taking sanctuary in
the sound of the hut's bell

– who's coming by
to find a bit of time?
the door is standing open
a hut's a state of mind

Girl in the Yard

What is she supposed to do?
She helps in the yard, mucks out,
takes her turn with his brothers

feeding the herd. Filches a jacket
off a scarecrow for him. No need,
he is cured hide already.

Cuts pigs with him. Herds
at sales, rides a wild pony for him
in front of sharp dealers.

They travel to the mart together,
drive the cattle-truck, sing
Take me back to the Black Hills...

Wears her cap at his angle.
Copies his whistle. Bids
for cockerels. His tomboy

milks cows alongside him
in the long byre. Walks with him
as his look-alike. Saw-partners

draw the two-handed saw,
ripping a kerf, each move
deepening the groove in logs.

What is she supposed to be?
His brothers turn the yard-hose
on her shirt cut from his cloth.

Reeds

I pull tall reeds for a child to take
from the mud shores of the Mugdrum
gathering a handful of cuts, razor nicks
                    lacerating finger and thumb.

Early this wintry morning we spread
our hands in the dew of the grass
on our way out of the reedbed
                    from estuary to terrace.

What Virgil did once for Dante
when he washed his face with dew
and plucked a reed belt for purgatory
                    up ahead, we do too.

Reeds we bring from the tide
spring from a new root
they wave by a child's side
                    move with a human foot

and tall as the sharp sea rush
long shadows cut out on our right
two men walking close by us
                    on the shoreline of light.

from *The Spring Teller* (2008)

Three Clootie Wells

for Roddy Mackenzie

1 St Mary's, Culloden Wood

Let the wandering begin here, at the well of youth
as night turns to day on the first Sunday in May
when the water becomes wine, for an instant. At first sight
a rag well with its crop of cloots, its colours always afloat
and airy above ground, seems a mango-tope with odd fruit,
golden orioles glancing through the grove, a strange tropic.

In the old birch wood, thickets of rags are tapestries
of ribbons, designer logo bows, baseball caps and mossy socks.
Tiny sisters, two blonde preschoolers, will show you how
to silver the water with a coin, to wish and keep it secret.
I tied up my baby blanket last year. I can tie knots!
Smaller and wiser than you. Leave a rag, lay trouble aside.

Winding wool around, stringing up J-cloths and mittens,
a throng are tying their pain up, each illness and circumstance.
As the nurse says of her patients, *You have to get to the knot.*
The story in the yarn tightens the cord of the universe.
When you look back, only one rag stirs, casting the colours
in the wood of silence and stillness. It's waving goodbye.

2 Munlochy

The trees stand knotting their neckties at the well's mirror,
in the deep dark sound of its water.
A pale young man is making three circuits
of the Hill o Hurdie, against the stream of crowds.
A Ross County sports jersey is strung between two trees
– the old hanging god.
T-shirts wrap trunks with marker messages:
I love you Big Time.
Black-clad teenage boys put up knee-pads like calloused skin,
bend under rag-laden boughs

where sickness and suffering hang and no-one touches those
or lets them brush against them.
Synthetic trainers dangle by a lace, grow slime-green.
Women hook a branch with a crook for yellow dusters: *There's your cloot frae last year, Jessie!*
No more room on this one! A wealthy matron,
Mercedes-borne, straddles the stream,
flicks her silk scarf to one side
and drinks – *Ah, delicious!*
A child leaves a poem written to the place.

A tiny doll hangs by the throat at the black well-mouth.
The weak thin young man descends, takes water from the trough,
and puts it on his chest. His wife seals that with a kiss.
He wears his hospital wristband.
People are getting over everything,
using these rip-rag gallows trees.
Flying between the traffic, the rags are filled with lost bodies
and as the wind blows it out, look, there's someone in the shirt!

3 Craigie Well

The well has a gurgling voice midway between man and bird
as the dawn wave of willow warblers ripples through the trees.
Hearing this spring is how they learnt their song as nestlings,
with the cadence of soft liquid notes, a lisping *hoo-eet*,
not loud but clear and carrying far into the distance.
So youngsters take into their being the sounds of May morning.

Round and down to the well on skiddy stones, new planks,
two little brothers in red tracksuits tie up their cloots,
take a sip and make their wish, everything done in order:
their mouths fill with water and with laughter.
A briar bush is clad in the coolest threads,
the spring is a bird slipping out of its nest.

Tobar Chragag, well of the little rock,
Craiguch, Craigack, Craigie,
chuckling, the chattering one,
chaffing, the laughing one,
escaping into the sun,
joy live with you, Craigie!

Frog Spring

Surprised by my tasting the spring, a golden frog
leaps to the bank. He flies to froggy places,
his ankle-joints stretch the moment.

A puddock from his pop-eyes to his paddle-toes,
he darts out of the vital pool. Immortal frog,
to see him so healthy is a sure sign

the spring will do the same for me.
He hops past my shoulder into the paddy-pipes,
the reed-bed pockets frog. He vanishes through,
each spear of rush keeps its own drop of dew.

The Green Well of Scotland

is a dragon-hoard, where once the wily Dr Dodds brought ore
from the gold-wells of Cairnsmore to mint West Indian coins:
then hid from the law, throwing his apparatus and the money
into this deep quarry-hole that has no outlet stream, only
something experimental boils up that breaks the glassy surface
with a low puff and fuffing.

From her sunning-spot
among the rocks an adder speaks her hissy *whihe* sound
with her big yellow mouth. Coils as thick as your wrist.
Red eyes draw a bead on you. Three forehead scales
are gold coins. She's going to the water to drink.
As she slips away, her impetus is all in her head.

Honeybee, Inner Hebrides

We sail to the Garvellachs with an autumn wind
along the string of islands. Heading out over the waves,
a honeybee lands on the guardrail of the yacht.
Ginger-brown and banded, he is a lost forager

who travels with us, resting to regain strength.
Where the gap is navigable, we put in at a place
of sheltered creek and grassy hollow. A few steps
and we drink at the miraculous well of sweet water

dashed by salt spray. The beehive cells nearby
are circles of stone, overlapping slabs, a domed roof.
It takes a whole rocky island to make a single drop
of honey. How far to fly? A solitary bee arrives

who grips the hazel-rod rim of a coracle, till he flies
up and off rapidly, to find the golden honeycomb.

Bernera Farm, Glenelg

Bernera, the glen of the gap,
is opening a break in space:
the spring full as a cup-mark
in its cylindrical concrete casing.
Now Anne MacRae has gone
with her brown blessed hand
that smelt of oiled rolled fleeces
and kept the well clean,
the trout, the guardian of the spring
has gone too, has disappeared.

The setting summer sun will light
on another young redhaired Anne
who wanders beside the hazel wood
below Cnoc a' Chomh-ruidh,
the rock of the running-together,
not long before her wedding.
She only has to gaze
beneath the surface for there to be
green and gold, with fine speckles,
a rare trout circling for a moment
revealing himself to her alone,
life-giving, boundary-crossing,
the fish in the well.

To Alexia

You stretch out your arms to me as I leave.
When you can walk further, I promise we'll go
together to the well in the field where I'll show
you how to keep it clear: a white quartz pebble
we'll give it, and a rhyme round as an egg.
A bright blue light on the wing, a kingfisher will fly
and the well-eye will open to your blue-green eyes.

Robert Burns' Mither at the Well

Grant's Braes, East Lothian

Ah'm gaun tae the well
wi ma stoups,
hummin a sang.
Mony words, muckle drouth.

Ah mind anither well
ayont the braes
years an years back
the length o Alloway.

Ma bairn at knee-hicht,
he wisna twa year auld,
paidlin in the well-strand,
crawin gey bauld.

He gied a first seuch
o fontal words
that flowed sae free,
like ony bird.

A clear mouth has aye
its well-heid.
Puir lad, he's awa
whaur the well's niver dry.

Heavenly Aqua

The low sun strikes with shattered light
across the tractor. Brimmed with gold,
his head looks as if he's wearing a halo.
'If I'd kent ye were comin I'd have
cleaned it oot for ye. It's no much
tae look at noo, it's all ochre. If I pour it
intae my whisky, it turns it green.'
A screed of rainbow oils on the surface
runs out of a D-basin, with waving
growths like oranges or Tibetan curds.
Dip a finger, it smells of rusty railings,
tastes of their corrugations. At the centre
of the moor is this heaven-sent chalybeate
whose iron in the water turns tea blue.

The World-Turtle

for St Anthony's Well, Arthur's Seat

They had no right
to seal up the well.
A great grey boulder
tries to drink
out of the stone basin.

When the world heats up,
the turtle who carries
the universe upon its shell
will turn over
and die of thirst.

Mermaid Pool

she's married to the farmer here
the wet edge of her apron betrays

how she loves to swim in the river
every day around noon

a naiad with no clothes on
a glimmering body of water

a whiteness swimming up
out of the deep pool on the bend

blonde tresses braid the current
her slit ears half-way in water

her soap-suds are the foam
on the reaches below Dod Mill

keep looking into the pool
and you will see her

but if she sees you first
she can take you with her

Mine Howe, Orkney

for Alistair Peebles, photographer

We are going into the pict-mirk.
We let ourselves down backwards,
holding onto a little thread
of light on the spiral stairway
that leads to the innermost darkness.

With shaky steps, toehold on treads,
the torch useless, our shoulders jam
against the walls, a pebble rolls
down past our hard hats
and rumbles into the hole below.

We hover on the half-landing
where a dog-skull guarded
the branching side-chambers.
One by one we enter the well.
Here's bodyroom enough for two,

a beehive chamber where we are held
in Mammy's Howe, the womb-house
with its neat channel drain for
the world-flood to pour away.
It's all around us.

You climb back up to the surface
and call down. If I can hear
your question, I must answer.
My hollow howe-speaking
mouth spouts off oracles,

tapping the spring to prophesy,
to find a way to avoid disaster.
From all the islands, people came
here to the oracle, they made it
so that we could become it.

The stair is a rush of warm air.
From the howe-dumb-dead depth,
drawn up the flight of steps
comes the sibyl, so withered
in the jar, only her voice is left.

Topopoems

Healing Well, Isle of Raasay

Don't think about it,
don't look for it,
that's how you'll find it
without searching the mountain

The Children's Well

To learn the time
of sea-tides,
the children watch the well
as it ebbs and flows

Pictish Well, Burghead

Massy on the headland,
a spring-fed cistern
big enough
to swim a bull in

Glen Mark

A sapphire on the moor
protruding from the glen's navel,
a gallus button winks up from the pool
in the centre of the bowl in the mountains

Chapel of Kilmore, Argyll

Walk up for a glimpse
of the two *mysticall fishes*:
the bow-waves of trout
hunting across the shallows

Robert Burns at the Brow Well

Suffering his last three weeks of fever,
he hoped to live, and drank from the *Bru*:
Burns seemed mortal then, he never knew
how mightily his hope was answered

Tobar Ashik, Isle of Skye

Bi glic! Bi glic! persist the oystercatchers.
Tobar Ashik absorbs our footsteps, grows quiet
as if it is listening, and recalling others from before:
after a moment or two, its clear sound flows on

St Bride's, Dunsyre

Drink and dream
how
Brigid hung her gown
on a sunbeam

St Medana's Well, Wigtownshire

Medana left Ireland and the man
who stalked her. Stepping onto a rock,
she floated here across the bay.
He followed, tried again to praise her.
She plucked her own eyes out,
You want these? He left unseen.

A disc of blue, the spring is flowing
beyond the boat-shaped rock
and its strand enters the salt sea.
This is where she washed her face
and somehow she could see again:
the painful stabs of sea-holly,

a rock-pipit on the cliff,
its streaked breast.
A tight cluster of sea aster
and a great mass of thrift.
Two perfect quartz pebbles
white and smooth as eyeballs.

Tobar a' Chinn, Glen Isla

Going up to the corrie, I rip my thin breeks
on a snaggle-toothed barbed wire fence.
By the tug of this path, the glen folk came
crowding with their rickety children for a cure.

Someone or something is watching me.
Maybe I'm in the orbit of rifle sights,
or of binoculars from a distant skyline,
or an eagle on wing above the mountain.

I look around to see who it can be.
Bottled-up, a purple orchid pouts its lower lip.
Toothy leaves of water avens nod their lanterns,
and cuckoo-flowers prick their round-lobed ears.

On the slope above me, the spring of springs
opens an eye, blinks through white chickweed.
The well of the head is talking, many voices
as one, speaking fluently all by itself.

Gougane Barra, West Cork

Lights shine all night on the island
And on the path, to help people do the rounds
In honour of St Finbar. Source of the Lee,
Your only place to be. The causeway runs out
Into the lake, a single swan preens its whiteness.

Coins have been plucked out of the tree
To let it live. Bright stream of the *slánán*,
Where bottles are filled with blackbird song.
Chill cell, whose dark dazzles. Prayers
Cell by cell fill the vault of each ribcage.

Bridegroom then bride arrive in fertile rain
To the sound of car radios. In its own self
The well is like nowhere else on earth.
Water kisses their mouths, intoxicates,
The strand repeats *this place, this space*.

Glencolmcille, Donegal

Strangers come here to make the long circuit of the glen
where its steep slope runs inland, drawing down the rain.
On the move, pilgrims will drink a sip of well water
and look through the holed stone to glimpse eternity.

I kneel in the wet hollow while a raven goes cronking over:
mountain and sky grow greater from the Place of the Knees.
To make three turns clockwise in the saint's flagstone bed
knocks shins, bruises ankles, presses the breast hard

by revolving: the stone pillow rattles beneath my head
and rocks me each time I surface looking skywards,
lips uttering prayers. Balancing, I face up the valley,

bare feet gripping the tippy Slab of Request: the mist
lifts from my heart. Strange, back in Scotland, pegging
out washing in a high wind, to feel so changed.

Uncollected Poems

The Sleepers

They worked a tracklife of fifty years,
These split logs lying under the rails,
Fixed on with cast-iron chairs
Spiked to their timber; sapside upward,
        Waybeams packed horizontal.

        Over the tracks run horses,
        Over the grass, the trains.
        Rivers rear in their courses,
        Sleepers rise, trees again.

The line's dismantled, section's down.
Imagining the future, a man stood
Here, thought another use could be found
For them, if he checked the timber's sound
        In close-grained wood,

Free from deadknots and warping shakes.
He tried the adzeing of the waney side,
How far the creosote impregnates,
What sawing and shifting it takes,
        What pitchpine can provide.

He stood the sleepers up on end,
Butted them together and secured
Those with nine-inch nails driven
Through. Doors and windows open
        At the fretsaw's signature.

He made the sleepers stable to a horse.
The big trees, heartside in, are joined.
Invert an opposite, move a force.
Emerging between standard-posts aligned,
                    The racer takes her living course.
As lightrays change, passing through a point,
                    The engine is antithesis of horse.

Over the tracks run horses,
Over the grass, the trains.
Rivers rear in their courses,
Sleepers rise, trees again.

To Edinburgh

Stone above storms, you rear upon the ridge:
we live on your back, its crag-and-tail,

spires and tenements stacked on your spine,
the castle and the palace linked by one rope.

A spatchcock town, the ribcage split open
like a skellie, a kipper, a guttit haddie.

We wander through your windy mazes,
all our voices are flags on the high street.

From the sky's edge to the grey firth
we are the city, you are within us.

Each crooked close and wynd is a busy cut
on the crowded mile that takes us home

in eden Edinburgh, centred on the rock,
our city with your seven hills and heavens.

Tipu's Amulet in Edinburgh Castle

He wore it on his upper arm, next his skin,
so there must be something in it.
He fastened the talisman of destiny to him,
never to be taken off. At the storming
of the fort, finding Tipu's body still warm,
Captain Young untied it from his arm.

Sewn up in flowered silk, a bubble
of brittle metal is hidden from sight.
With its Arabic manuscript, the flat capsule
slides around as if alive, inside.
The blowers on knots chant powerful words,
musk in the ink and a sharp Persian sword.

Given to wear with love, no amulet
is a piece of dead matter, cold, inert.
How many times can it protect? Two
musket-balls passed through his chainmail shirt.
A stolen amulet, losing its active powers,
can withhold them from its new owner.

Overgrown with jungle, the old Gajalhatti Pass
still shows what's called *Tipu's Road* in places.
His amulet harms no-one. The angel's writing
is shut up among crowded gems in glass cases.
This is one relic which can restore
a hero, a future, to the state of Mysore.

Short Poems

stormy morning
the tenements stand still
the sun zips about

we go walking
only one shadow
cast on the wall

Mairi's flightcase
is heavy with one
stone from the island

April
apparition

mavie sang
tillieloot tillieloot tillieloot

Jackpot 4th Leg

Two tube journeys and a bus to 'Walfhamstow'.
You'll love that – the East End,
no tourists, a *Racing Post* under your arm.
The stadium is huge and white,
the track is sand and grit.

An electric hunting horn winds on tape,
the greyhounds emerge through the gates
led by a huntsman in bowler and black jacket.
Handlers walk in red. Dogs pee.
They've been crated for hours.

White, blue, racing colours parade past the stands.
The big fawn dog pricks his ears, the silver bitch
looks fit and happy. One minute left to bet.
They yelp in the traps. The hare comes round
doing 50mph, a silly little toy

with a flapping scarf and orange jacket.
They're off! The one who caught the eye
is quick away, she's running a blinder.
Another meets bad trouble at the bends,
baulked and badly bumped, hits the fence.

But the silver whelp of August 97,
she shows pace down the back straight
to pass her rivals, runs on well,
stretching in the air at the finish,
the track gouged by clawmarks.

Funny Wink
in great form, loves having her photograph taken

Blue Hackle
stays well enough, punish any mistakes up front

Saltee Wind
caused a shock last time, needs a swift exit

Megs Enry
well drawn, will be staying on along the rails

Silverhill Gina
will make them all go if popping out those boxes

Select Issue
only a puppy, will be better than these in time

Walking up to Compline in the Rain

walking up to Compline in the rain
by the curving path to the rounded archway
with wooden gate and handworn stile

through the booming of the monks' bees
and under the hum note of the bell
to where psalms lap the shore of lips

et sub alas ejus confugies
the arc of the sunset clouds
western wing of a flying angel

in pace simul ac decubui obdormisco
monks from the garden with hoods up
golden peas in open pods

I kneel to chestnut carving and to spirit
at the window to the lady chapel
o clemens o pia o dulce Virgo Maria

where the dove lights on the white
halo of a maiden mother
standing on a silver crescent moon

she holds her child on her right arm
and apostles wake, gold haloes slipping
a wild gust of wind sweeps by

in manus tuas they're singing when
my feet standing on stone floor pavings
are suddenly – not standing on anything

the life of love continuing
in the tender last hymn of the monks
salve regina... the gate is everywhere

all the colourful faces and figures
I am getting to know well
friends and brothers in the doorway

watch two monks ring the bells
passing over a rope, a single toll
– follow the sound into the great silence

Flora of the Forest

brancHes
rArely
Welcomed
inTo
Houses
tabOo
foRbids
garlaNds

Crataegus monogyna

Flora of the Garden

sPinning
clOwning
Petal
Plates
giddY-making

Meconopsis sheldonii

Ravendean Burn

Just knowing he's out there is enough.
A far-away bird flies with the black clouds.

Then a noise like no other you'll ever hear:
a throat-singer from the steppes, a pig-snort,

a star-burst, a log-pile rolling, cork-drawing pops,
body-blow drums, horses' hooves on a hard road.

This is sooo raven. He comes cronking over
to speak to you. He likes to *toc* the *toc*.

Anything with a vocal edge goes down well
with him. *Prruk prruk. Krroak krronk.*

Toc toc toc. Corvus corax corax. Corbie-
quirky breakbeats all the way, gruff barks.

The ravens are returning to Ravendean,
the black one roosts on White Craig,

new birds on the ancestral crag. He feeds
the young ravens who cry out to him.

The Roman augurs would be prophesying
with these cries of *korp korp* from his axe-bill.

He's sporting his thunderhead today, sings
his raven-praise of storm-winds, flips over

till he flies upside-down, turns iridescent,
now beats his direct flight into the distant hills.

Romanno Terraces

The drag and drop of step-like terraces
Write lines to us in wintry black on white
With their steep risers and narrow treads,
Ribbed slits and scoops of light.

Early cultivation is a line of cut,
A row of turf-seats, grassy scalps,
A slice of this slope raised up
Tiny field by field, alp by alp.

Their flight of steps, time's escalator
On the face of a hill with an outward curve.
Come down, come down, ancestors, spectators
Watching us, we know when we're observed.
Our children are getting used to going away,
The future will arrive unexpectedly.

Wedding in Stobo Kirk

A song thrush calls
clear among the hills,
with his recurring note
the rounded archway fills.

The bride who walks sunwise
up the path to the kirk door
brings a ray of light,
snowy foot on cobbled floor.

A flower on her golden head
by the stone-cut floret passes,
the stirring of a breeze
along the hilltop grasses.

Where the bridegroom waits
he has, for guard of honour,
two-handed sword, rowel spurs,
a carved warrior in armour.

From a very early time
love comes to live with them
by the wedding-kiss,
the blossom on the stem.

By the blessing of the rings,
two ripples in the pool,
a bride and bridegroom meet
as good as they are beautiful.

Love follows in the footsteps
of the constant and the leal:
those who came here before,
they are just as real.

For a thousand years and more,
voice to voice, their vows,
and for all those yet to come,
love is living in the now.

Through the green wood of Stobo
in the month of May
these two will go
to live and love always.

Saint Andrew, Patron of Scotland

Andrew was a fisherman
    the first called by Christ
the first to follow him
    into the light.

In a Greek port
    his bones lay at rest.
An angel shone, saying
    'Take his relics west

to divide and share him
    through the world now
like the loaves and fishes
    passed round the crowd.'

So a wandering boat
    put in from the sea
with a cross of clouds
    to guide our country,

a saltire in the sky,
    white on blue.
The king gave the place
    to God and Saint Andrew.

A finger of his hand
    is touching Scotland –
awake, awake
    for Saint Andrew's sake!

Fieldwalkers

Today's hunter-gatherers
have an eye for the land
they can add up all the years
of fieldwalking together
the sum of their experience
with each companion

The little terracotta
head of Minerva
wearing her wisdom-helmet
and giving a quizzical look –
Walter remembers finding her
and crossing the field to Mason
Is this anything?

then the whole way back
Mason cupped her head in his hands
looking into her face

Meadow Brown

On sunny days she's always on the wing
dusky brown   autumn brown
she delights in open ground

She's agile over hedge and scrub
cocoa brown   mocha brown
she delights in open ground

How fast she flies in upland meadows
brindle brown   bracken brown
she delights in open ground

She skims the moorland and the downs
fuscous brown   fawn brown
she delights in open ground

The Harp to Aeolus

Inscription for the Wind-Harp by Mark Norris,
installed in the Royal Botanic Gardens Edinburgh

North wind to the hills
sounding the storm

East wind to the waves
cold blows along

South wind to the elm-seeds
wings flying on

West wind to our loved ones
bringing them home

A Year as an American Bird

Mount Auburn Haiku

Ruby-crowned kinglet
hover-gleans the flies off
a biker jacket

The northern goshawk,
rare bird on a branch:
a snowman in a tree

Red cardinals whistle
on cue, cue, cue:
Who're you?

Mockingbirds
check, check
you out

A voice from dense wood:
Hey, a Canada warbler
comin up yor way!

He bathes in a pool
with low buzzing sound:
each feather kissing water

Savannah sparrows,
one fluffing out his crisp streaks
in the open

The hermit's fluty
ethereal song –
speckles in deckled paper

The great horned owl
roosts,
one among spruce boughs

The bush sparks off
parula warblers –
so quick, so blue, so orange

The red-tail hawk flies over
where she is sleeping:
his shadow wakes her

Bobbing along wires,
the jay is jockeying
for the best place

The father points up,
the child sees orange, O!
– orchard oriole

A house finch
in rosy-feathered dawn
blows you a raspberry

Flying solo,
solitary vireo –
chu-wee cheerio

Who owns this big dog?
– coyote running
carrying prey

An eastern screech-owl
keeks out her tree-trunk roost-hole:
feisty foxy red

From among the leaves,
How's my crest looking today?
a tufted titmouse

A fall evening:
the spotted sandpiper
ready to fly

Aubade for Mount Auburn

A stranger is welcome to these paths, to follow
Shadow wood, shadow wind, over hill or hollow,

Wandering among trees and birds who bless
The bourne of golden-brown, a slope of openness.

Birdsong begins in the pure realm of sound:
As the sun comes up, their singing resounds

Through these glowing trees, awake with the dawn,
The glories of the sky where the future will form.

Peter Pan Shadow

As if stitched to flying feet
leaping out across continents
o lengthening shadow you have
come to this clump of switch grass
topped by tall seed heads
with its blades that break you up
into your many shapes
opening out all the hidden places
no-one else has been to
and its leaves are already turning
blood-red in the fall so this
is the moment you know why
your grandfather showed you
how to slit a blade of grass
and whistle through the space

Song Sparrow

Little streaked ground
feeder loves to hop around
these grassy mounds

low brushy leas
then suddenly
flies up into the tree

puts back his head and bursts
out into song – bosky husky
the short notes first

with one long trill to
zieeeeee he's telling you
something *tipo zeet zeet* new

The Vanishing Whip-poor-will

I used to hear him all the time
whip-puwiw-weew
more often heard than seen

calling his name, jarring the night
tuck-whip-puwiw-weew
a mottled brown moth in flight

I think I can hear him sometimes
whip-puwiw-weew
rolling out to his goatsucker kind

tonight it's only in my mind

Bird Lady

Sonia the birder, full of years and songs,
        a tiny figure
        in a quilted coat,
        sturdy brown brogues,
        bright coloured hat,
she wears her binoculars with verve.

From deep in the snows of winter I hear her,
        'I'm on my way out...
        but I've been saying that
        for the last two hours.'
She calls an ID and a direction for me
and continues to call till I have the sighting.

World-watcher, what will be her life-list,
        that all-species ID
        in the life of one person
when she reaches her century of sun, rain, cold and wind?

We're birding the spring migration in Mount Auburn
when out of the sky a palm warbler flies straight to us:
        I put out my finger,
        he thinks about landing,
        then flies onto her head.
'If you love them, they come close,' she says,
        'I love them
        and I bless them,
I say to them, *Have a good life!*

And I have been blessed by *them*.'

The Whisper Song

So very noisy, usually,
with those harsh screams,
he sits all alone,
perched among the first buds.

His blue crest is slicked back,
a dark necklace lies on his breast,
at peace with the world,
whispering away to himself.

The most raucous bird
becomes the most subtle.
He sings under his breath,
runs through the repertoire:

the squeaky-gate calls,
the rapid repeats,
the whirring and mewing
gentle as a kiss.

He is fluffed up, content,
musing on his subsong.
Few have heard
the whisper of the blue jay.

The Sang o the Swamp Angel

Aye bird alane, bird alane
aye hale heartit
lilt liltin thrissel-cock

clair awa, faur awa
threip threip threipin
at creek-o-day clamant

lumen luminar, locus lovabill
wheeple whauple
ane tryst-o-truith truly

licht lichtsome day-daw
dysart days-licht lustral
aye halie halie morn-ie-morning

zhweeee

swamp angel: the American hermit thrush

A Northern Parula Blown to the Hebrides

Wee bluachie, blown across the sea,
you're not where you hoped to be,
in American woods near fresh water.
Weirdie, transatlantic vagrant warbler,
your blue head is draigled by the storm,
sharp-nebbit with this under-orange,
your yellow throat ruffled up the wrong way.
White wing-bars skim the crests of waves
when a stray wind takes you to North Uist.
Your flight-call falls, a high descending *zip*.
A pale arc shows, a trace within your eye,
how you just dropped out of the sky.

Cody Dancing

A boy in a sleeveless tee, his pale torso
twisted to one side, pushes his metal
walker frame ahead of him. He drags crumpled
feet across the grassy powwow ground.

Spurred by the drums, he joins in
every one of the dances: the Smoke Dance,
the Sneak-Up Dance, the Honor Dance.
Falling, he is helped up on his feet again.

A medicine man steps alongside him,
passes the wing-feather of a golden eagle
over and above him as he reels
through the long day in hot sun.

Someone puts a war-bonnet on his head
to show who he really is. And now
the sky-being soars. Still dancing, Cody
is called up for the money prize.

George Washington's Feather War Helmet

A young Hawaiian chief wore this
in procession through the streets
after disembarking from the first
Boston ship to sail right around the Pacific.
He saw the city while he remained unseen.

The prow of this war helmet curves
over the brow with a clutch of feathers,
a head-gear of plumes to flutter in the wind:
the head-dress takes on bird powers,
the beauty of eye and feather on the wearer.

A crest of red and cream is jutting
out beyond the frontlet, at one with the birds.
The basket-work netting of the cap
is completely covered in feathers:
one bird is extinct, out of the two used.

Given to George Washington, did he try it on?
America's crown has many feathers.
So what happened to that young man?
Did he return to the Pacific?
Invisible, he's hiding behind the birds.

Eagle Bone Whistle

The eagle wing-bone
worked into a whistle
with a single hole
is hung from a thong
whipped with bird quills.
The shrill wheep
of spirit flows through the bone
the whish of a wing
moving fast through the air,
a Mandan war whistle
to breathe through,
to breathe through
wheeeooo
wheeeooo
wheeeooo

The Raven Regalia

Airborne
the black-painted
warrior who moves
tail-feathers fanning out to launch
birdman

skimming
iridescence
bustle of quills and fur
beaks and tails worn into battle
alive

raven
regalia
become feather rosettes
shining on men who dance today's
powwow

Ode to the Sacred Pipe

Wherever it appears
is a place of great presence.
It is sacred
even to see one.
The pipe-stem of the calumet
is longer than arm's-length,
a hollow path for the smoke,
a pipe feathered
for a new alliance.

Seven blotched tail feathers
of the young bald eagle
threaded through porcupine quills:
they can expand,
a fan unfolds,
the air stirs,
an eagle takes wing,
chief of the sky.

Six beaks and scalps
of pileated woodpeckers
bend over backwards,
wrapped along the stem:
that warlike drummer-bird
will not be so angry.
One beak
of the ivory-billed woodpecker,
chief of the forest.

Orange-dyed horsehair
of different horses;
a coppery plume
of wild hemp,
tied on with red trade wool;
braided sweetgrass
with the imprint
of the fingers that rolled it,
the grass that never breaks.

Summer thunder,
lightning stroke
over mountains and valleys,
visions and faces
with a pipe to share.

A passport through strange lands
where smoke curling up
brings two peoples
together,
and the breath of the pipe
joins the future
of our children
in ways
we could never
guess.

Some other books published by **LUATH PRESS**

The Spring Teller

Valerie Gillies

ISBN 978-1-906307-76-9, PBK £12.99

Every spring has its own song: volatile and bubbling or deep and dramatic. The sonic signatures of dark underground wells, forceful mountain springs or hidden inner city wells are recorded in poetry.

The Spring Teller is a poetic journey to lost springs and legendary sources, medieval well-houses and healing waters. Meeting animal guardians and human well-keepers, or being asked to use the power of words to unlock urban wells, Valerie found that the element of water remains as miraculous as it has ever been.

This collection captures a moment in the flowing stream. With photographs and a map pinpointing the locations of springs and wells, the reader too can discover the joy of well-hunting.

Gillies' poetry shows a masterly fluency with form kept taut by its over-riding themes... this is polyglot poetry, yet it has a remarkably unbookish and outdoors feel. SB KELLY, SCOTLAND ON SUNDAY

Men & Beasts: Wild Men and Tame Animals of Scotland

Valerie Gillies

ISBN-978-0-946487-92-9, PBK, £15.00

Travel across Scotland with poet Valerie Gillies and photographer Rebecca Marr: share their passion for a land where wild men can sometimes be tamed and tame beasts can get really wild.
Among the wild men they find are a gunner in Edinburgh Castle, a Highland shepherd, a ferryman on the River Almond, an eel fisher on Loch Ness, a Borders fencer, and a beekeeper on a Lowland estate. The beasts portrayed in their own settings include Clydesdale foals, Scottish deerhounds, Highland cattle, blackface sheep, falcons, lurchers, bees, pigs, cashmere goats, hens, cockerels, tame swans and transgenic lambs.

Valerie Gillies is one of the most original voices of the fertile avant-garde Scottish poetry. MARCO FAZZINI, l'Arco, Italia

The work of Valerie Gillies and Rebecca Marr is the result of true collaboration based on insight, empathy and generosity. JULIE LAWSON, *Studies in Photography*

Details of books published by Luath Press can be found at:

www.luath.co.uk

Luath Press Limited

committed to publishing well written books worth reading

LUATH PRESS takes its name from Robert Burns, whose little collie Luath (*Gael.*, swift or nimble) tripped up Jean Armour at a wedding and gave him the chance to speak to the woman who was to be his wife and the abiding love of his life. Burns called one of the 'Twa Dogs' Luath after Cuchullin's hunting dog in Ossian's *Fingal*. Luath Press was established in 1981 in the heart of Burns country, and is now based a few steps up the road from Burns' first lodgings on Edinburgh's Royal Mile. Luath offers you distinctive writing with a hint of unexpected pleasures.

Most bookshops in the UK, the US, Canada, Australia, New Zealand and parts of Europe, either carry our books in stock or can order them for you. To order direct from us, please send a £sterling cheque, postal order, international money order or your credit card details (number, address of cardholder and expiry date) to us at the address below. Please add post and packing as follows: UK – £1.00 per delivery address; overseas surface mail – £2.50 per delivery address; overseas airmail – £3.50 for the first book to each delivery address, plus £1.00 for each additional book by airmail to the same address. If your order is a gift, we will happily enclose your card or message at no extra charge.

Luath Press Limited
543/2 Castlehill
The Royal Mile
Edinburgh EH1 2ND
Scotland
Telephone: +44 (0)131 225 4326 (24 hours)
email: sales@luath. co.uk
Website: www. luath.co.uk